ST. PAUL

LIBRARY

ELEMENTARY

Take a trip to
SYRIA

Keith Lye

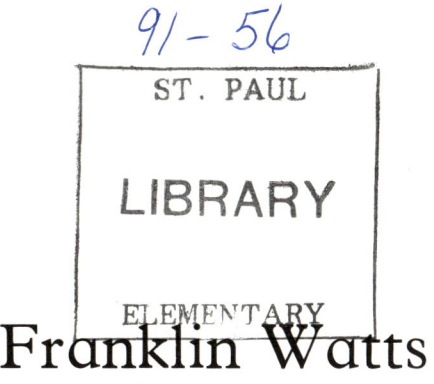

Franklin Watts
London   New York   Sydney   Toronto

Facts about Syria

Area:
185,180 sq. km
(71,498 sq. miles)

Population:
10,931,000

Capital:
Damascus

Largest cities:
Damascus (1,251,000)
Aleppo (977,000)
Homs (355,000)
Latakia (197,000)
Hama (177,000)

Official language:
Arabic

Religion:
Islam

Main exports:
Oil, textiles, tobacco, cotton, fruit, and vegetables

Currency:
Syrian pound

Franklin Watts
12a Golden Square
London W1

Franklin Watts Inc.
387 Park Avenue South
New York, N.Y. 10016

ISBN: UK Edition 0 86313 721 0
ISBN: US Edition 0 531 10560-1
Library of Congress Catalog
Card No: 87-51699

Typeset by Ace Filmsetting Ltd.,
Frome, Somerset
Printed in Hong Kong

© Franklin Watts Limited 1988

Maps: Simon Roulstone

Design: Pritilata Chauhan

Stamps: Harry Allen International Philatelic Distributors

Photographs: Chris Fairclough, 8; Hutchinson Library, 5, 6, 10, 12, 13, 16, 17, 18, 19, 21, 22, 23, 24, 25, 26, 27, 28, 29, 30, 31; Jenny Pate, 4; Jamie Simson, 3, 7, 15; Zefa, 11, 14, 20

Front Cover: Zefa
Back Cover: Jamie Simson

The Syrian Arab Republic is a country in southwestern Asia. Its chief port on the Mediterranean Sea is Latakia, shown here. Syria was important in ancient times. The coastal region of Syria was once part of Phoenicia. This civilization traded with ancient Egypt more than 4,000 years ago.

East of the coastal plains are hills and mountains. The highest mountains are the Anti-Lebanon Mountains on the border with Lebanon. The coastal plains and the western slopes of the mountains get plenty of rain. The eastern slopes are much drier.

Hama is a city on the Orontes River. Huge waterwheels lift water from this river to irrigate farmland. The Orontes valley is Syria's most fertile region. About 80 per cent of Syria's people live in the west, on the coastal plains, in the mountains, or in the river valleys.

Eastern Syria gets little rain. The region contains large areas of dry grassland and desert. Desert covers about a fifth of the country. Winters are mild in Syria but summers are hot, except in the highest mountains.

The Euphrates River and its tributaries flow across northeastern Syria. The river valleys are irrigated. A dam has been built across the Euphrates. Behind it, water is stored in a large reservoir called Lake Assad.

The picture shows some stamps used in Syria. The main unit of currency is the Syrian pound, which is divided into 100 piastres.

About nine out of every ten Syrians speak Arabic. The Kurds in the north make up about six per cent of the population. Kurds, who have their own language and culture, are also found in Iran, Iraq and Turkey. Some Kurds want to establish their own country.

Besides Arabs and Kurds, Syria has several other small groups of people, including Armenians. There are also a few nomadic herders called Bedouins. Some groups are descended from ancient peoples. Aramaic, the language spoken by Jesus and his disciples, is still spoken in some villages.

Some important early civilizations were founded in Syria. One was Ebla in northern Syria. This major kingdom existed between 2700 and 2200 BC. The people of Ebla spoke a language which was similar to ancient Hebrew. Historians are still digging up the ruins of Ebla.

Syria has been conquered many times. It became part of the Persian empire in about 500 BC, but it was taken by the Greeks in 333 BC. The Romans occupied Syria in 64 BC. The Romans turned the old settlement of Palmyra into a desert fortress. Impressive Roman ruins still stand there.

Damascus is one of the world's oldest cities. It stands on an oasis in southwestern Syria. It was probably founded about 5,000 years ago. Some old buildings survive, but most of Damascus today is modern. About half of Syria's people live in cities and towns.

Muslim Arabs took Damascus in AD 635. It became one of the chief cities in the Muslim empire. Arabic became Syria's main language and Islam its chief religion. The mosque in the picture is in Aleppo, Syria's second largest city after Damascus.

In 1095, Christian Crusaders began a series of wars aimed at regaining the Holy Land from the Muslims. They built some magnificent castles in Syria. The Crac des Chevaliers, shown here, is a Crusaders' castle west of Homs. But the Muslims finally triumphed in the wars and held Syria.

Aleppo is almost as old as Damascus. When the Turks took over Syria in 1516, they rated Aleppo as the third most important city in their empire after Constantinople (now Istanbul) and Cairo. The Turks ruled Syria until World War I. France ruled Syria from 1920 until Syria's full independence in 1946.

Damascus is the capital of the Syrian Arab Republic, as the country is officially called. The Head of State, the President, is also head of the government. The country has an elected People's Council.

The President of Syria since 1971 has been Lieutenant-General Hafiz al-Assad. His photograph (the man with the moustache in this picture) is a common sight in Damascus. Assad is leader of the socialist Baath party.

Syria opposed the founding of Israel in 1948. It has been involved in wars with Israel. Israel has occupied the southwestern corner of Syria. This region, called the Golan Heights, stretches as far as Mount Hermon, Syria's highest peak.

Farmland, including dry grassland, covers 77 per cent of Syria and farming employs 32 per cent of Syria's workers. Wheat is the main food crop. Most farms are privately owned. Many are worked by hand. Farm machinery is used on the few large government-owned farms.

Cotton is Syria's chief crop apart from wheat. Raw cotton and textiles are important exports. The country's leading resource and export is oil. Syria ranks seventh among the oil producers of southwestern Asia.

Vegetables, including squash grown here on irrigated land near Aleppo, are important foods in Syria. Other food crops are beans, fruits and onions. There are many food processing industries in the cities.

Sheep and goats are raised on dry grasslands. Most of these animals are owned by nomadic peoples who drive their flocks to places where they expect to find some pasture at certain times of the year.

The huge Tabka Dam on the Euphrates River holds back Lake Assad. At the dam are hydroelectric plants. They produce seven-tenths of Syria's electricity. The economy of Syria is much less developed than most Western countries.

Syria has many craft industries, and its workers produce beautiful metalwork and textiles. Cement, glass, soap and tobacco products are also made. The main industrial cities are Damascus, Aleppo, Homs and Latakia.

The ways of life of people in country areas of Syria have changed little over hundreds of years. In the northwest, many people live in beehive-shaped houses made of mud. In the south and east, many houses are made of stone.

Many country people wear long robes and headdresses to protect themselves against the sun and wind-blown dust. Family life is important in Syria. Grandparents usually live with their children and grandchildren. The picture shows women making carpets.

Many people in the cities wear western clothes. But cloth head coverings are still common. Bread is the main food, together with vegetables, dairy products and fruits. Lamb is popular, but poor people eat meat only on special occasions.

Beautiful tapestries are common decorations in homes in the country and city areas. Living standards are gradually rising and educational services are improving. About half of Syria's people can read and write.

Syria is a mixture of old traditions and modern ideas. Women once occupied a low place in society. But their position is changing because of education and western ideas. Today about a third of Syria's university students are women.

Index

Aleppo 15, 17
Anti-Lebanon Mountains 4
Arabic 15
Aramaic 11
Armenians 11
Assad, Lake 7
Assad, Lt.-Gen. H. al- 19

Climate 4, 6
Clothes 28–29
Cotton 22
Crac des Chevaliers 16
Crusades 16

Damascus 14–15, 18

Ebla 12
Education 30–31
Electricity supply 25
Euphrates River 7, 25
Exports 22

Family life 28
Farming 21–24
Food 29

Golan Heights 20
Government 18–19

Hama 5

Hermon, Mount 20
History 12–17
Homes 27, 30

Industries 26
Irrigation 5, 7
Islam 15

Kurds 10

Languages 10–11
Latakia 3

Mediterranean Sea 3

Oil production 22
Orontes River 5

Palmyra 13
Phoenicia 3

Sheep 23
Squash 23
Stamps 8

Tabka Dam 25
Textiles 28, 30

Wheat 21

ST. PAUL
LIBRARY
ELEMENTARY

DATE DUE

MAY 2 6			
MAR 1 8			
JAN 1 1			

Demco, Inc. 38-293